For my daughter Hollie
You have been through more than most
I dedicate this book to you and Wanda
Much love xx

100% of the profits from every book sold will be donated to
Flynn's Legacy helping families who suddenly lose a child on a farm
www.flynnslegacy.com

Wanda
Written by Laura O'Neill
Illustrated by Laura O'Neill

Copyright 2025 Laura O'Neill
All rights reserved. No part of this book may be reproduced
in any manner whatsoever without prior written
permission of the publisher.
First printing 2025
Published by Laura O'Neill

ISBN 978-1-7641742-0-6

The sun had risen
at the little cottage
down the lane
The sunflowers
beamed
after a long week of
rain

Hollie lay in her bed all toasty and warm
as she rubbed her eyes and let out a yawn
The kookaburra's sung their sweet singing tune
while they chorused away the night time moon
The air was warm and the skies were clear
as Hollie smelt adventure in the air

Hollie cuddles his bear as her tears
roll to the floor
Her tummy fills with sadness
as her memories hit her core

She missed her big brother
and the joy he brought her days
As she felt her life had changed
in so many ways

She missed their days together and the
games they used to play
He used to call me girl in his own special way

She wiped her tears away as
she couldn't help but hear
This really strange scratching
which sounded quite near

She grabbed her hat and
popped on her boots
As she bolted like a bronc
being let from the chutes

As she neared the back door
Hollie slowed her pace
She didn't want it startled
so she slowed down the race

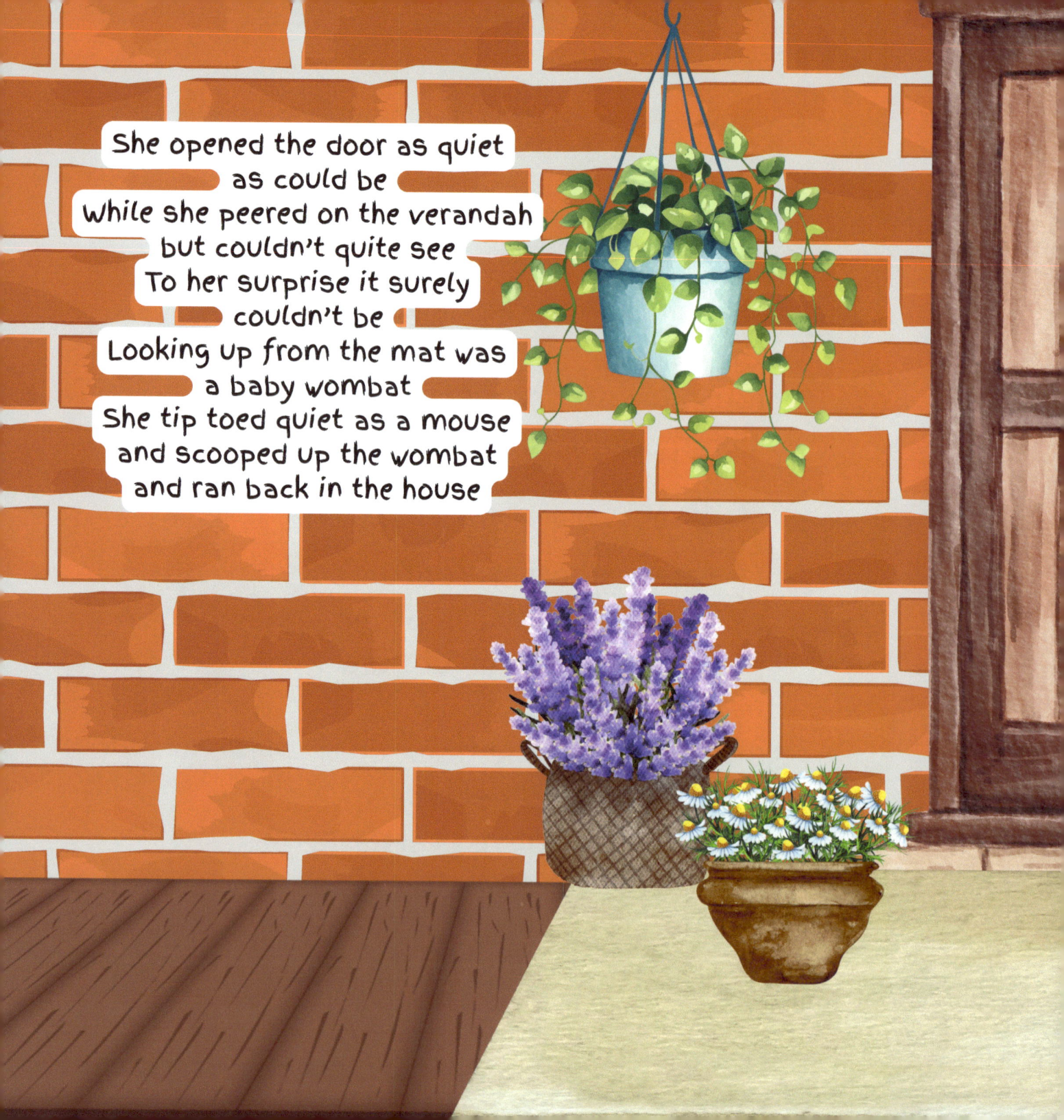

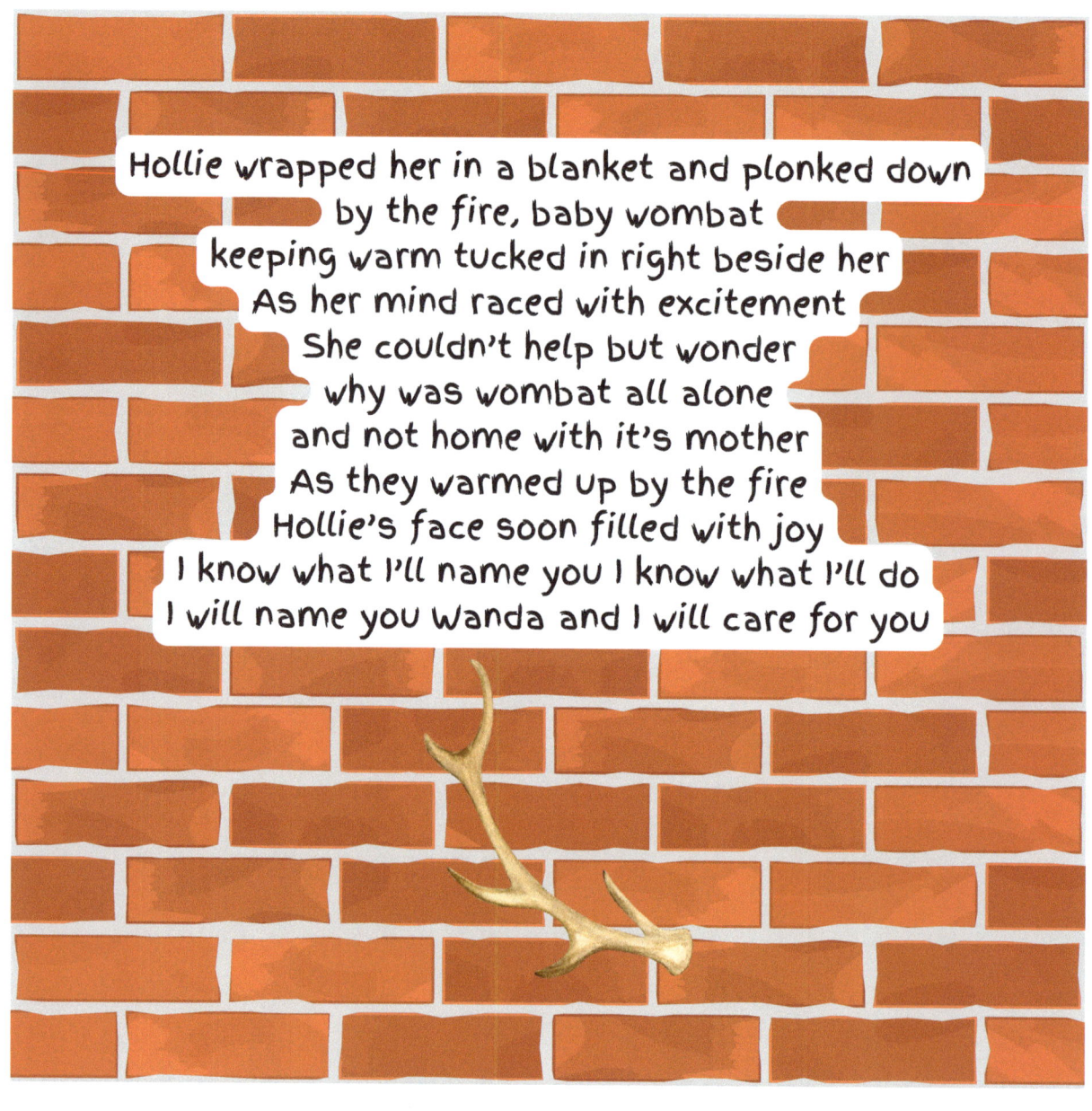

Their days were filled with love and
joy as they spent their time
exploring
Running, laughing, dancing
as they played the days away
This bond they shared was special
as they helped each other heal
Hollie for her brother while Wanda
missed her mother
They took each others pain away
as they took care of each other
As the seasons started changing
and the leaves had stopped
their fall
Their sadness slowly faded
as they found joy after all

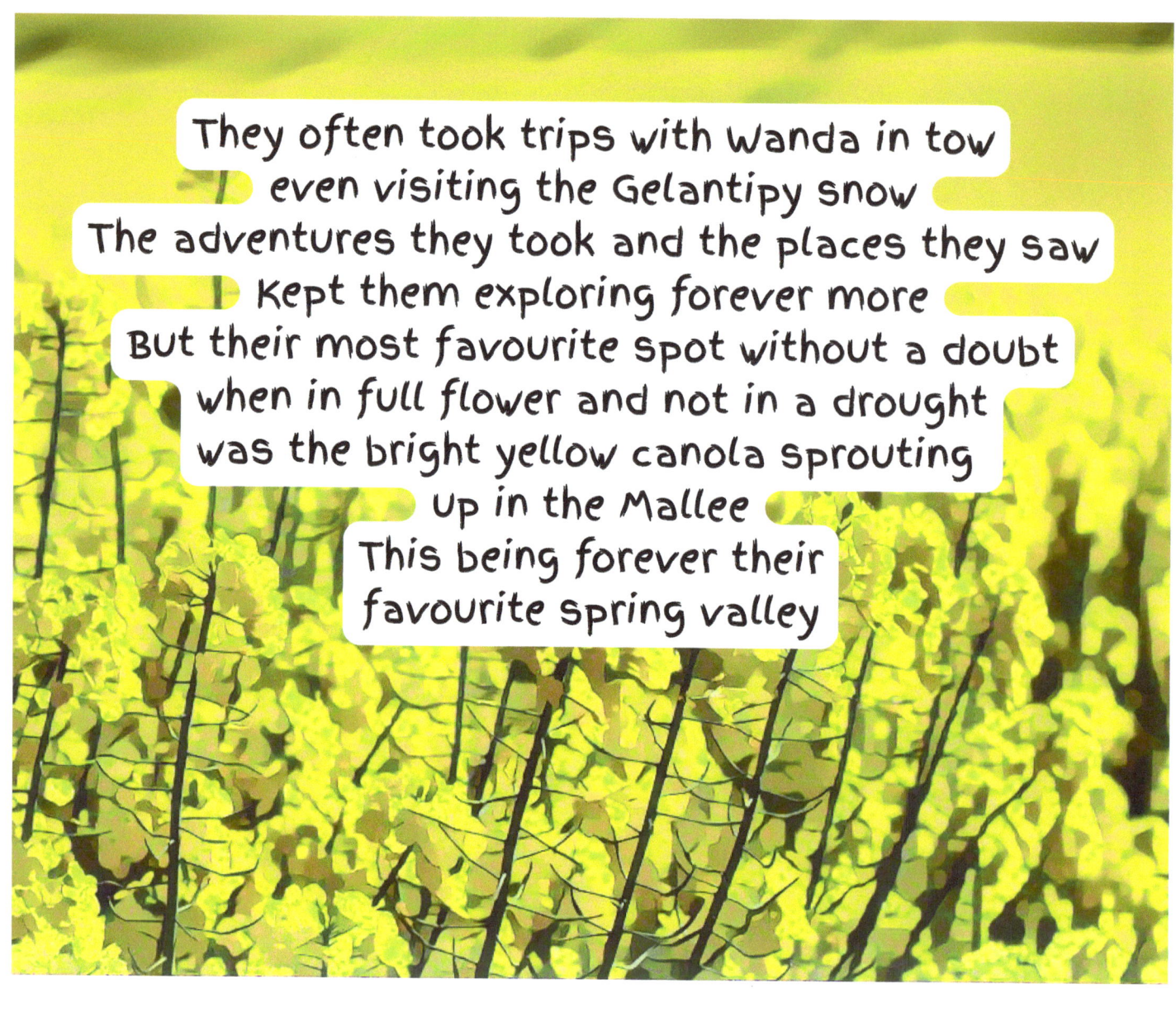

They often took trips with Wanda in tow
even visiting the Gelantipy snow
The adventures they took and the places they saw
Kept them exploring forever more
But their most favourite spot without a doubt
when in full flower and not in a drought
was the bright yellow canola sprouting
up in the Mallee
This being forever their
favourite spring valley

As the harvest season approached
Goondiwindi called their name
As the family headed North
on their annual harvest claim
Goodbyes can be tricky and make us feel quite sad
But Wanda while we're gone
You can be free and nomad
We'll be back before you know it just you wait and see
We will be together just you and me

The harvest run was bountiful
with trucks and crops galore
Their time in Gundi over now
They headed for the shore
The family stopped and felt the sand
and played amongst the waves
As they gathered the momentum
to head home to Buchan Caves

With the Kenworth home and bags unpacked
The team reunited and made a pact
Wanda loved her home but she needed to roam
Hollie loved her friend and never wanted it to end
So the pact was decided right there and then
Wanda would wombat and visit her friend

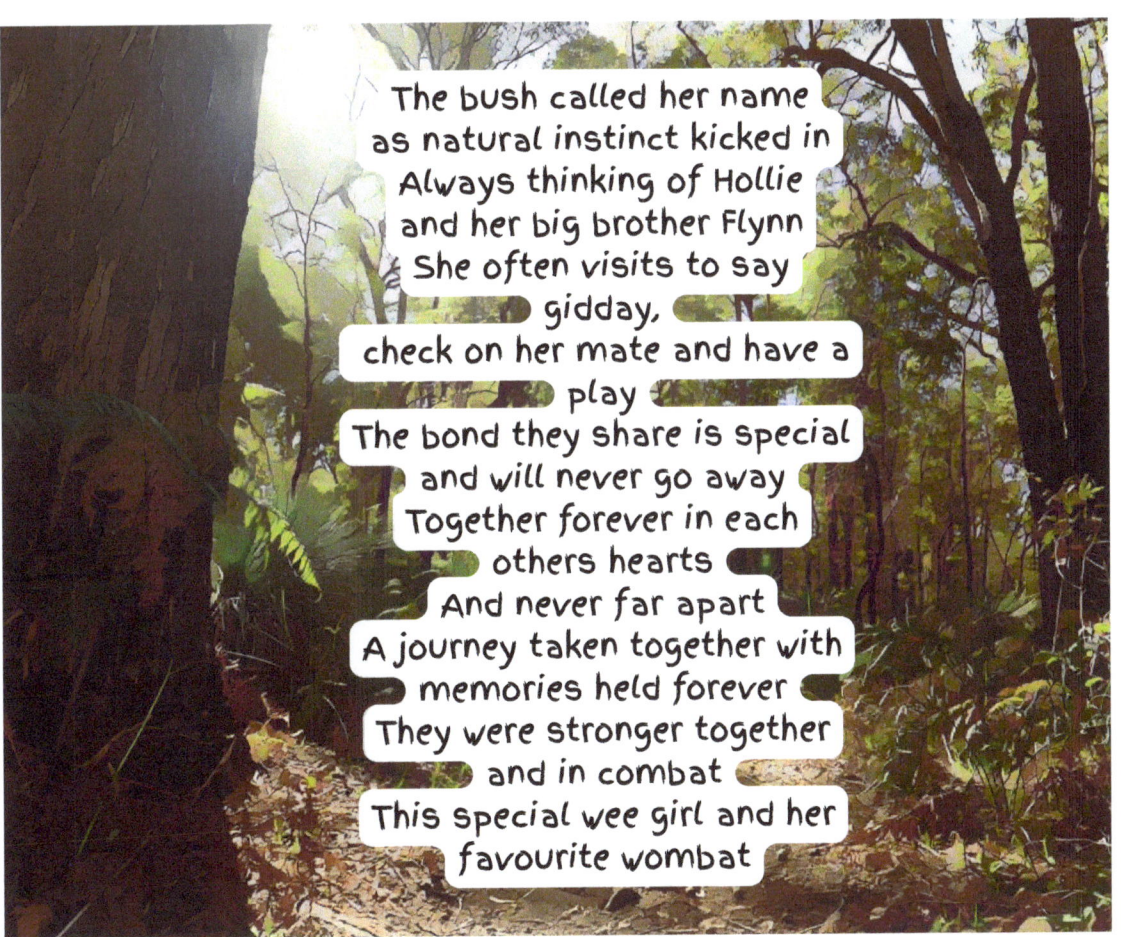

The bush called her name
as natural instinct kicked in
Always thinking of Hollie
and her big brother Flynn
She often visits to say gidday,
check on her mate and have a play
The bond they share is special
and will never go away
Together forever in each others hearts
And never far apart
A journey taken together with
memories held forever
They were stronger together
and in combat
This special wee girl and her
favourite wombat

www.ingramcontent.com/pod-product-compliance
Lightning Source LLC
Chambersburg PA
CBHW041503220426
43661CB00016B/1234